Activating God's Power

in Justin

by Michelle Leslie

Activating God's Power

Copyright © 2015 Michelle Leslie

All rights reserved.

ISBN: 978-1-68193-186-9

Michelle Leslie

DEDICATION

For Justin

Activating God's Power

Michelle Leslie

CONTENTS

Activating God's Power in Your Life and in Others'	1
Anxiety	3
Blessing & Favor	6
Calling	11
Character	15
Direction	17
Discernment	19
Discipline	21
Encouragement	23
Faith	25
Family	28
Fear	31
Forgiveness	33
Freedom	34
Grace	36

Healing	37
Hope	41
Humility	43
Identity	44
Joy	46
Love	47
Obedience	48
Peace	50
Perseverance	52
Prayer	55
Promise	57
Provision	58
Purity	60
Redemption	62
Revelation	63
Righteousness	65
Safety & Protection	67
Salvation	70
Seeking God	72

Spiritual Growth	75
Spiritual Warfare	77
Strength	81
Transformation	85
Trials	87
Trust	88
Wisdom	89
Worship	91
Author's Note	92
Testimony	93
About the Author	95
Contact	97

Activating God's Power

Michelle Leslie

ACKNOWLEDGMENTS

Thank you to God, my family, mentors, friends, and neighbors for all your love and support as God prepared me to put this book together.

May the Lord bless you and keep you, the Lord make His face shine upon you and be gracious to you; the Lord turn His face toward you and give you peace.
Numbers 6:24

Activating God's Power

Michelle Leslie

ACTIVATING GOD'S POWER IN YOUR LIFE AND IN OTHERS'

Sometimes we don't know what or how to pray, but we are in need of God's power in our lives. When we pray God's word we can never pray outside God's will for our lives or the lives of others. When we meditate on the word and speak it we are activating God's power. God's word brings life and creates a spiritual mindset that changes us and the world around us (Romans 12:2).

There are many great books on overcoming addiction, having a successful marriage, being effective in ministry, overcoming anxiety, or being a great parent. I challenge you that the solution to all of the above is God's word. There is no formula to solve these issues, but the word of God is alive (Hebrews 4:12) and can empower you to do and be what God is calling you or others to do and be in any circumstance. It transforms the heart and the mind. The word of God brings clarity and strength.

However different from person to person, we all have challenging circumstances and personal weaknesses to overcome. God tells us in the book of Ephesians to use His word (the sword of the Spirit) to fight these battles. We will overcome and will be transformed when we access God's power available in His word. Jesus says in John 8:31-32, "If you abide in my word, you are truly my disciples, and you will know the truth, and the truth will set you free."

God's power is available to each one of us. Activate His power in your life and in the lives of those around you. Speak it, personalize it, and let the power of God transform your life and circumstances.

Anxiety

Justin is strong and courageous. Justin is not afraid or terrified because the Lord his God goes with him; He will never leave him nor forsake Justin."

Deuteronomy 31:6

The Lord goes before Justin and is with him; He will never leave Justin or forsake him. Justin is not afraid or discouraged.

Deuteronomy 31:8

Justin fears no evil because the Lord is with him; God's word and Spirit comfort Justin.

Psalm 23:4

Justin casts his burdens on the Lord, and He sustains him; He will never permit the righteous to be moved.

Psalm 55:22

Anxiety

"Justin comes to me when he labors and is heavy laden, and I give him rest. Justin takes my yoke upon him, and learns from me, for I am gentle and lowly in heart, and he finds rest for his soul. For my yoke is easy, and my burden is light."

Matthew 11:28-30

Peace I leave with Justin; my peace I give to him. Not as the world gives do I give to Justin. Justin lets not his heart be troubled, neither does he lets his heart be afraid.

John 14:27

Justin rejoices in the Lord always and lets his gentleness be evident to all. The Lord is near to Justin so he is not anxious about anything, but in every situation, by prayer and petition, with thanksgiving, he presents his requests to God. And the peace of God, which transcends all understanding, guards Justin's heart and mind in Christ Jesus.

Philippians 4:4-7

Anxiety

Justin casts all his anxiety on Him because He cares for Justin.

1 Peter 5:7

When Justin lies down, he will not be afraid; when Justin lies down, his sleep will be sweet. Justin has no fear of sudden disaster or of the ruin that overtakes the wicked, for the Lord is at his side and will keep his foot from being snared.

Proverbs 3:24-26

Activating God's Power

Blessing & Favor

May the Lord bless and keep Justin; the Lord make His face to shine on Justin and be gracious to him; the Lord turn His face toward Justin and give him peace.

Numbers 6:24-26

As Justin listens to these commands of the Lord and is careful to obey them, the Lord will make Justin the head and not the tail, and Justin will always be at the top and never at the bottom.

Deuteronomy 28:13

"Oh, that You would bless Justin indeed, and enlarge Justin's territory. May Your hand be with Justin, and keep Justin from evil, that it may not cause him pain.

1 Chronicles 4:10

You gave Justin life and showed him kindness, and in your providence You watch over his spirit.

Job 10:12

Michelle Leslie

Blessing & Favor

May the favor of the Lord our God rest on Justin; and establish the work of Justin's hands—yes, establish the work of Justin's hands.

Psalm 90:17

For You bless the righteous, O Lord; you cover Justin with favor as with a shield.

Psalm 5:12

You prepare a table before Justin in the presence of his enemies; you anoint his head with oil; Justin's cup overflows. Surely goodness and mercy shall follow Justin all the days of his life, and he shall dwell in the house of the Lord forever.

Psalm 23:5-6

Justin is like a tree planted by streams of water that yields its fruit in its season, and its leaf does not wither. In all that Justin does, he prospers.

Psalm 1:3

Blessing & Favor

Justin is blessed because he fears the Lord; he greatly delights in His commandments. Justin's descendants will be mighty on earth; the generation of the upright will be blessed.

Psalm 112:1-2

For the Lord God is Justin's sun and shield; the Lord bestows favor and honor on Justin; no good thing does He withhold from Justin whose walk is blameless.

Psalm 84:11

"Justin's wife shall be like a fruitful vine in the very heart of his house, his children like olive plants (a symbol of anointing) all around his table."

Psalm 128:3

Michelle Leslie

Blessing & Favor

"For I will pour water on Justin when he is thirsty, and floods on the dry ground; I will pour My Spirit on Justin's descendants, and My blessing on Justin's offspring; they will spring up among the grass like willows by the watercourses.

Isaiah 44:3-5

"For I know the plans I have for Justin," declares the Lord, "plans to prosper Justin and not to harm him, plans to give Justin hope and a future."

Jeremiah 29:11

Thank you Lord that it will come to pass that You will pour out Your Spirit on Justin; Justin shall prophesy, dream dreams, and see visions.

Joel 2:28

Activating God's Power

Blessing & Favor

The heart of Justin is like good soil; he hears the word, accepts it, and produces a crop—some hundred times that which he has sown.

Mark 4:20

He who supplies seed to the sower and bread for food will supply and multiply Justin's seed for sowing and increase the harvest of his righteousness.

2 Corinthians 9:10

Calling

The Lord makes firm the steps of Justin who delights in Him.

Psalm 37:23

Your word is a lamp to Justin's feet and a light to Justin's path.

Psalm 119:105

Justin trusts in the Lord with all of his heart. Justin leans not on his own understanding; in all Justin's ways he acknowledges God and God directs Justin's path.

Proverbs 3:5-6

In his heart Justin plans his course, but the Lord establishes Justin's steps.

Proverbs 16:9

Calling

"For I know the plans I have for you Justin," declares the Lord, "plans for you to prosper and not to harm you, to give you a future and a hope. Then Justin will call upon me and come and pray to me, and I will hear him. Justin will seek me and find me, when Justin seeks me with all of his heart."

Jeremiah 29:11-13

God's gifts and His call on Justin are irrevocable.

Romans 11:29

May the eyes of Justin's heart be enlightened, that he may know what is the hope to which He has called him, what are the riches of His glorious inheritance in the saints.

Ephesians 1:18

Justin lives a life worthy of the calling he has received.

Ephesians 4:1

Calling

He who began a good work in Justin will be faithful to complete it.

Philippians 1:6

For it is God who works in Justin to will and to act in order to fulfill His good purpose.

Philippians 2:13

With this in mind, we constantly pray for Justin, that our God may make Justin worthy of His calling, and that by His power He may bring to fruition Justin's every desire for goodness and deed prompted by faith.

2 Thessalonians 1:11

He has saved Justin and called him to a holy life—not because of anything he has done but because of His own purpose and grace.

2 Timothy 1:9

Calling

When Justin lacks wisdom, he asks God, who gives generously to all without reproach, and it is given to him.
James 1:5

Justin is diligent to confirm his calling and election. As Justin practices these qualities he will never fall.
2 Peter 1:10

Character

Justin's integrity and uprightness protect him, because Justin's hope, Lord, is in you.

Psalm 25:21

Justin does not walk in the counsel of the ungodly or stand in the path of sinners or sit in the seat of scoffers. But Justin delights himself in the law of the Lord and Justin meditates on His law day and night. Justin is like a tree planted by the rivers of water, which yields its fruit in season and whose leaf will not wither, and whatever he does he prospers.

Psalm 1:1-3

Justin walks with integrity; his children are blessed after him.

Proverbs 20:7

Justin is concerned about the Lord's affairs; his aim is to be devoted to the Lord in both body and spirit.

1 Corinthians 7:34

Character

Justin is very careful how he lives—not as unwise but wise, making the most of every opportunity.

Ephesians 5:15-16

God, as one of Your chosen people, holy and dearly loved, help Justin to clothe himself with compassion, kindness, humility, gentleness, and patience.

Colossians 3:12

Justin shows proper respect to everyone. Justin loves the family of believers, fears God, and honors the emperor.

1 Peter 2:17

Direction

Your word is a lamp to Justin's feet and a light to Justin's path.

Psalm 119:105

He refreshes Justin's soul. He guides Justin along the right paths for His name's sake.

Psalm 23:3

"I will instruct Justin and teach him in the way he should go; I will counsel Justin with my eye upon him."

Psalm 32:8

The Lord's angels keep charge over Justin to guard him in all his ways.

Psalm 91:11

The Lord makes firm the steps of Justin, who delights in Him.

Psalm 37:23

Direction

In his heart Justin plans his course, but the Lord establishes Justin's steps.

Proverbs 16:9

Justin trusts in the Lord with all of his heart. Justin leans not on his own understanding; in all Justin's ways he acknowledges God and God directs Justin's path.

Proverbs 3:5-6

The Lord will guide Justin always; He will satisfy Justin's needs in a sun-scorched land and will strengthen Justin's frame. Justin will be like a well-watered garden, like a spring whose waters never fail.

Isaiah 58:11

Discernment

Justin, do not forget my teaching, but let your heart keep my commandments, for length of days and years of life and peace they will add to you. Let not steadfast love and faithfulness forsake you, Justin; bind them around your neck; write them on the tablet of your heart. So you will find favor and good success in the sight of God and man. Trust in the Lord with all of your heart, and do not lean on your own understanding.

Proverbs 3-6:35

Justin does follow the Good Shepherd and Justin knows His voice, and the voice of a stranger Justin will not follow.

John 10:4-5

Justin does not conform to the pattern of this world, but he is transformed by the renewing of his mind. Justin is able to test and approve what God's will is—His good, pleasing and perfect will.

Romans 12:2

Discernment

And this is my prayer: that Justin's love may abound more and more in knowledge and depth of insight, so that Justin may be able to discern what is best and may be pure and blameless for the day of Christ.

Philippians 1:9-10

Justin tests everything. Justin holds on to what is good. Justin avoids every kind of evil.

1 Thessalonians 5:21-22

But solid food is for the mature. By constant use Justin has trained himself to distinguish good from evil.

Hebrews 5:14

Discipline

Justin does not let the book of the Law depart from his mouth. Justin meditates on it day and night. Justin is careful to do everything written in it, so he will be prosperous and successful.

Joshua 1:8

Justin hides God's word in his heart so he is careful to not sin against Him.

Psalm 119:11

Blessed is Justin whom You discipline, O Lord, and You teach Justin out of Your law, to give Justin rest from days of trouble. For the Lord will not forsake Justin; He will not abandon Justin's heritage.

Psalm 94:12-14

Justin does not run aimlessly; he does not fight like a boxer beating the air. But Justin disciplines his body and keeps it under control.

1 Corinthians 9:26-28

Discipline

Justin lives by the Spirit, and does not gratify the desires of sinful nature.

Galatians 5:16

Justin does not let the sun go down on his anger, and he does not give the devil an opportunity.

Ephesians 4:26

Justin does not regard lightly the discipline of the Lord, nor is he weary when reproved by Him. For the Lord disciplines the one He loves, and chastises every child whom He receives.

Hebrews 12:5-6

Michelle Leslie

Encouragement

May the God who gives endurance and encouragement give Justin a spirit of unity with others as he follows Christ Jesus.

Romans 15:5

Justin has encouragement from being united with Christ. Justin has comfort from His love, fellowship with the Spirit, His tenderness and compassion. Justin's joy is complete because he is like-minded with Christ and has the same love and is one with Christ in spirit and purpose. Justin does nothing out of selfish ambition or vain conceit, but in humility, Justin considers others better than himself and looks to the interests of others. Justin's attitude is the same as that of Christ Jesus.

Philippians 2

Encouragement

Justin is encouraged in heart and united in love. Justin has the full riches and complete understanding of the mysteries of God, namely Christ, in whom are hidden all the treasures of wisdom and understanding.

Colossians 2

Faith

Therefore I tell you, whatever Justin asks for in prayer, he believes that he has received it, and it will be his.

Mark 11:24

Faith comes from hearing, and hearing through the word of God. Justin's faith increases every time he hears or reads the word of God.

Romans 10:17

For it is with Justin's heart that he believes and is justified, and it is with his mouth that Justin professes his faith and is saved.

Romans 10:10

Faith

Justin does not lose heart. Though outwardly he is wasting away, yet inwardly Justin is being renewed day by day, for Justin's light and momentary troubles are achieving for him an eternal glory that far outweighs them all. So Justin fixes his eyes not on what is seen, but what is unseen, since what is seen is temporary, but what is unseen is eternal.

2 Corinthians 4:16-18

Justin has been crucified with Christ. Justin no longer lives, but Christ lives in him. The life Justin now lives in the body, he lives by faith in the Son of God, who loved him and gave Himself for him.

Galatians 2:20

Faith

For it is by grace Justin has been saved, through faith—and this is not from yourselves, it is the gift of God—not by works, so that no one can boast. For Justin is God's handiwork, created in Christ Jesus to do good works, which God prepared in advance for Justin to do.

Ephesians 2:8-10

Justin knows that the testing of his faith produces perseverance.

James 1:3

Though Justin has not seen Him, he loves Him; and even though Justin does not see Him now, he believes in Him and is filled with an inexpressible and glorious joy, for Justin is receiving the end result of his faith, the salvation of his soul.

1 Peter 1:8-9

Family

Justin prayed for his child, and the Lord has granted him what he asked of Him.

1 Samuel 1:27

Justin is blessed because he fears the Lord; he delights greatly in His commandments. Justin's descendants will be mighty on earth; the generation of the upright will be blessed.

Psalm 112:1-2

"Justin's wife shall be like a fruitful vine in the very heart of his house, his children like olive plants (a symbol of anointing) all around his table."

Psalm 128:3

Justin walks with integrity; his children are blessed after him.

Proverbs 20:7

Family

Justin has been trained up in the way he should go; and when he is old, he will not depart from it.

Proverbs 22:6

"For I will pour water on Justin when he is thirsty, and floods on the dry ground; I will pour My Spirit on Justin's descendants, and My blessing on Justin's offspring; They will spring up among the grass like willows by the watercourses.

Isaiah 44:3-5

Thus says the Lord: "Justin restrains his voice from weeping, and his eyes from tears; for his work shall be rewarded," says the Lord, "They shall come back from the land of the enemy. There is hope in Justin's future," says the Lord, "That your children shall come back to their own border."

Jeremiah 31:16-17

Family

Justin obeys his parents in the Lord. Justin honors his father and mother so that it may go well with him and that Justin may enjoy long life on earth.

Ephesians 6:1-3

Fear

Justin is strong and courageous. Justin is not afraid or terrified because the Lord his God goes with him; he will never leave him nor forsake Justin.

Deuteronomy 31:6

The Lord goes before Justin and is with him; He will never leave Justin or forsake him. Justin is not afraid or discouraged.

Deuteronomy 31:8

Justin fears no evil because the Lord is with him; God's word and Spirit comfort Justin.

Psalm 23:4

When Justin lies down, he will not be afraid; when Justin lies down, his sleep will be sweet. Justin has no fear of sudden disaster or of the ruin that overtakes the wicked, for the Lord is at his side and will keep his foot from being snared.

Proverbs 3:24-26

Fear

"Justin fears not, I am with him; Justin is not dismayed, for I am his God; I will strengthen Justin, I will help him, I will uphold Justin with my righteous right hand."

Isaiah 41:10

Justin rejoices in the Lord always and lets his gentleness be evident to all. The Lord is near to Justin so he is not anxious about anything, but in every situation, by prayer and petition, with thanksgiving, he presents his requests to God. And the peace of God, which transcends all understanding, guards Justin's heart and mind in Christ Jesus.

Philippians 4:4-7

Justin casts all his anxiety on Him because He cares for Justin.

1 Peter 5:7

Michelle Leslie

Forgiveness

As far as the east is from the west, so far has He removed Justin's transgressions from him.
Psalm 103:12

Justin loves his enemies; he does good to those who hate him.
Luke 6:27

Justin forgives, as the Lord has forgiven him.
Colossians 3:13

"Justin's sins and lawless acts I will remember no more."
Hebrews 10:17

Activating God's Power

Freedom

Out of Justin's distress he called on the Lord; the Lord answered Justin and set him free.

Psalm 118:5

Justin will know the truth, and the truth will set Justin free.

John 8:32

So if the Son sets Justin free, Justin will be free indeed.
John 8:36

Justin is dead to sin but alive to God in Christ Jesus.
Romans 6:11

Justin has the right to do anything, but not everything is beneficial to him. Justin has the right to do anything, but he will not be mastered by anything.

1 Corinthians 6:12

Freedom

It is for freedom that Christ has set Justin free. Justin stands firm, then, and does not let himself be burdened again by a yoke of slavery.

Galatians 5:1

Justin was called to freedom. Justin does not use his freedom as an opportunity for the flesh, but through love he serves others.

Galatians 5:13

In Him and through faith Justin approaches God with freedom and confidence.

Ephesians 3:12

Justin lives as a person who is free, not using his freedom as a cover-up for evil, but living as a servant of God.

1Peter 2:16

Grace

God's grace is sufficient for Justin, for His power is made perfect in weakness.

2 Corinthians 12:9

He who began a good work in Justin will be faithful to complete it.

Philippians 1:6

For it is God who works in Justin to will and to act in order to fulfill His good purpose.

Philippians 2:13

Grace and peace be Justin's in abundance through the knowledge of God and of Jesus our Lord. His Divine Power has given Justin everything he needs for a godly life through his knowledge of Him who called Justin by His own glory and goodness.

2 Peter 1:2-3

Healing

Justin serves the Lord his God, and He blesses his bread and his water. He will take sickness away from him.

Exodus 23:25

O Lord my God, Justin cries to You for help, and You have healed him.

Psalm 30:2

Justin blesses the Lord with all his soul, and forgets not all His benefits, who forgives all his iniquity, who heals all his diseases.

Psalm 103:2-3

He sent out His word and healed Justin, and delivered him from his destruction.

Psalm 107:20

Healing

Justin shall not die, but he shall live, and recount the deeds of the Lord.

Psalm 118:17

He heals Justin's broken heart and binds up his wounds.

Psalm 147:3

Justin is not wise in his own eyes; he fears the Lord, and turns away from evil. It is healing to his flesh and refreshment to his bones.

Proverbs 3:7-8

Justin pays attention to what I say; he turns his ear to my words. Justin does not let them escape from his sight; he keeps them within his heart. For they are life to Justin and healing to his flesh.

Proverbs 4:20-22

Healing

He was pierced for Justin's transgressions; He was crushed for his iniquities; upon Him was the chastisement that brought Justin peace, and with His wounds he is healed.

Isaiah 53:5

Then Your light will break forth like the dawn, and Justin's healing will quickly appear; then Your righteousness will go before Justin, and the glory of the Lord will be his rear guard.

Isaiah 58:8

Heal Justin, O Lord, and he shall be healed; save Justin, and he shall be saved, for You are Justin's praise.

Jeremiah 17:14

"Take heart, Justin; your faith has made you well."

Matthew 9:22

Healing

And these signs shall follow Justin, who believes; in Christ's name he shall cast out devils; he shall speak with new tongues; he shall pick up serpents; and if he drinks any deadly thing, it shall not hurt him; he shall lay hands on the sick, and they shall recover.

Mark 16:17-18

And the prayer of faith will save Justin when he is sick, and the Lord will raise him. And if he has committed sins, he will be forgiven.

James 5:15

He Himself bore Justin's sins in His body on the tree, that Justin might die to sin and live to righteousness. By His wounds Justin has been healed.

1 Peter 2:24

Justin, I pray that all may go well with you and that you may be in good health, as it goes well with your soul.

3 John 1:2

Hope

"For I know the plans I have for you Justin," declares the Lord, "plans to prosper you and not to harm you, to give you a future and a hope. Then Justin will call upon me and come and pray to me, and I will hear him. Justin will seek me and find me, when Justin seeks me with all of his heart.

Jeremiah 29:11-13

Justin hopes in the Lord and the Lord renews his strength. Justin will soar on wings like an eagle. Justin will run and not grow weary. Justin will walk and not be faint.

Isaiah 40:31

Justin knows that in all things God works together for the good of those who love Him, and have been called according to His purpose.

Romans 8:28

Hope

May the God of hope fill Justin with all joy and peace in believing, so that by the power of the Holy Spirit Justin may abound in hope.

Romans 15:13

Justin is joyful in hope, patient in affliction, faithful in prayer.

Romans 12:12

Justin rejoices in his sufferings, knowing that suffering produces endurance, and endurance produces character, and character produces hope, and hope does not put Justin to shame, because God's love has been poured into his heart through the Holy Spirit who has been given to him.

Romans 5:3-5

Humility

Justin does not think of himself more highly than he ought, but rather he thinks of himself with sober judgment, in accordance with the faith God has distributed to him.

Romans 12:3

Justin does nothing out of selfish ambition or vain conceit, but in humility he doesn't consider himself better than others. Justin does not only look out for his own interests, but also the interests of others. Justin has this mindset which was also in Christ Jesus.

Philippians 2:3-5

Justin humbles himself before the Lord, and the Lord will lift Justin up.

James 4:10

Justin humbles himself under God's mighty hand, that He may lift him up in due time.

1 Peter 5:6

Identity

Before God formed Justin in the womb He knew him; before Justin was born He set him apart.

Jeremiah 1:5

Justin is united with the Lord and is one with Him in spirit.

1 Corinthians 6:17

Justin has been crucified with Christ. Justin no longer lives, but Christ lives in him. The life Justin lives in the flesh he lives by faith in the Son of God, who loved him and gave himself for him.

Galatians 2:20

Justin is God's workmanship, created in Christ Jesus to do good works, which God created in advance for Justin to do.

Ephesians 2:10

Identity

God, as one of Your chosen people, holy and dearly loved, help Justin to clothe himself with compassion, kindness, humility, gentleness and patience.

Colossians 3:12

The Spirit of the Lord is upon Justin because He has anointed Justin to preach the good news to the poor. He has sent Justin to bind up the brokenhearted, to proclaim freedom for the captives and release from darkness for the prisoners, to proclaim the year of the Lord's favor and the day of vengeance of our God. Justin comforts those who mourn, and provides for those who grieve in Zion. Justin bestows on them a crown of beauty instead of ashes, the oil of gladness instead of mourning and a garment of praise instead of the spirit of despair.

Isaiah 61:1-3

Joy

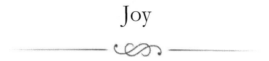

Justin does not grieve, for the joy of the Lord is Justin's strength.

Nehemiah 8:10

The Lord is Justin's strength and shield; Justin's heart trusts in him, and he helps Justin. Justin's heart leaps for joy, and with a song Justin praises him.

Psalm 28:7

Though Justin has not seen Him, he loves Him; and even though Justin does not see Him now, he believes in Him and is filled with an inexpressible and glorious joy, for Justin is receiving the end result of his faith, the salvation of his soul.

1 Peter 1:8-9

Love

Justin loves the Lord with all of his heart, and with all of his soul, and with all of his strength.

Deuteronomy 6:5

Justin's love prospers; he is forgiving. Justin never dwells on a fault because it can separate close friends.

Proverbs 17:9

May Justin have power, together with all of the Lord's holy people, to grasp how wide and long and high and deep is the love of Christ.

Ephesians 3:18

And this is my prayer: that Justin's love may abound more and more in knowledge and depth of insight, so that Justin may be able to discern what is best and may be pure and blameless for the day of Christ.

Philippians 1:9-10

Obedience

As Justin listens to these commands of the Lord, and is careful to obey them, the Lord will make Justin the head and not the tail, and Justin will always be at the top and never at the bottom.

Deuteronomy 28:13

Justin walks in obedience to all that the Lord his God has commanded him, so that he may live and prosper and prolong his days in the land that he will possess.

Deuteronomy 5:33

Justin seeks You with all his heart; Justin will not stray from Your commands; Justin has hidden Your word in his heart that he may not sin against You.

Psalm 119:10-11

Obedience

Justin does not walk in the counsel of the ungodly or stand in the path of sinners or sit in the seat of scoffers. But Justin delights himself in the law of the Lord and Justin meditates on His law day and night. Justin is like a tree planted by the rivers of water, which yields its fruit in season and whose leaf will not wither, and whatever he does he prospers.

Psalm 1:1-3

Justin obeys his parents in the Lord. Justin honors his father and mother so that it may go well with him and that Justin may enjoy long life on earth.

Ephesians 6:1-3

Justin is a doer of the word, not a hearer only, deceiving himself.

James 1:22

Peace

Great peace has Justin, who loves your law, and nothing can make him stumble.

Psalm 119:165

Justin is kept in perfect peace. Justin's mind is steadfast, because he trusts in You.

Isaiah 26:3

Great is the peace of Justin, for he is taught by the Lord.

Isaiah 54:13

Justin will go out in joy and be led forth in peace; the mountains and hills will burst into song before him, and all the trees of the field will clap their hands.

Isaiah 55:12

Peace

Jesus left Justin with a gift: peace of mind and heart. And the peace Jesus gave isn't like the peace the world gives. So Justin is not troubled or afraid.

John 14:27

Justin is not anxious about anything, but in everything by prayer and supplication with thanksgiving he lets his requests be made known to God. And the peace of God, which surpasses all understanding, guards Justin's heart and mind in Christ Jesus.

Philippians 4:6-7

Perseverance

Justin will not be overcome by evil circumstances. Justin will be long remembered. Justin does not fear bad news; he confidently trusts the Lord to care for him.

Psalm 112:6-7

Justin rejoices in his sufferings, because he knows that suffering produces perseverance, perseverance produces character, and character hope, and hope does not disappoint us.

Romans 5:3-4

Justin knows that in all things God works together for the good of those who love Him, and have been called according to His purpose.

Romans 8:28

Perseverance

Forgetting what is behind, and straining toward what is ahead, Justin presses on towards the goal to win the prize for which God has called him heavenward in Christ Jesus.

Philippians 3:13-14

Justin rejoices always, prays continually, and gives thanks in all circumstances; for this is God's will for Justin in Christ Jesus.

1 Thessalonians 5:16-18

Justin never tires of doing what is good.

2 Thessalonians 3:13

Justin does not throw away this confident trust in the Lord. Justin is richly rewarded. Justin patiently endures, so that he will continue to do God's will. Then Justin will receive all that he has been promised.

Hebrews 10:35-36

Perseverance

Perseverance is finishing its work in Justin. Justin is mature and complete in Christ, not lacking anything. Justin asks God for wisdom and God gives Justin wisdom generously without finding fault.

James 1:4-5

Justin counts it all joy, my brothers, when he meets trials of various kinds, for he knows that the testing of his faith produces steadfastness. Justin lets steadfastness have its full effect, so that he may be perfect and complete, lacking in nothing.

James 1:2-4

In this Justin greatly rejoices, though now for a while he may have to suffer grief and all kinds of trials. These have come so that his faith—of greater worth than gold, which perishes even though refined by fire—may result in praise, glory and honor when Jesus Christ is revealed.

Peter 1:6-7

Prayer

Justin prayed for his child, and the Lord has granted him what he asked of Him.

1 Samuel 1:27

Justin cries out, and the Lord hears, and delivers him out of his troubles.

Psalm 34:17

Justin calls upon God, and the Lord saves him. Evening, morning, and at noon, Justin will pray and cry aloud, and God hears his voice. God has redeemed Justin's soul in peace from the battle waged against him.

Psalm 55:16-18

And this is the confidence that Justin has toward Him, that if he asks anything according to His will He hears him.

1 John 5:14

Prayer

The Spirit helps Justin in weakness; for although Justin may not know how he should pray, the Spirit Himself intercedes for Justin with groanings too deep for words; and he who searches our hearts knows what the mind of the Spirit is, because He intercedes for Justin according to the will of God.

Romans 8:26-27

Justin rejoices always, prays without ceasing, gives thanks in all circumstances; for this is the will of God in Christ Jesus for him.

1 Thessalonians 5:16-18

With confidence Justin draws near to the throne of grace, that he may receive mercy and find grace to help him in time of need.

Hebrews 4:16

Justin casts all his cares on God because He cares for Justin.

1 Peter 5:7

Promise

Justin has been trained up in the way he should go; and when he is old, he will not depart from it.

Proverbs 22:6

"And I will give Justin a new heart, and a new spirit I will put within him. And I will remove the heart of stone from Justin's flesh and give him a heart of flesh. And I will put my spirit within Justin, and cause him to walk in my statutes and he will be careful to obey my rules."

Ezekiel 36:26-27

He who began a good work in Justin will be faithful to complete it.

Philippians 1:6

As Justin draws near to God, God draws near to Justin.

James 4:8

Provision

The Lord is Justin's shepherd; Justin lacks nothing.
Psalm 23:1

The lions may grow weak and hungry, but Justin seeks the Lord and lacks no good thing.
Psalm 34:10

For the Lord God is Justin's sun and shield; the Lord bestows favor and honor on Justin; no good thing does He withhold from Justin whose walk is blameless.
Psalm 84:11

The Lord will guide Justin always; He will satisfy Justin's needs in a sun-scorched land and will strengthen Justin's frame. Justin will be like a well-watered garden, like a spring whose waters never fail.
Isaiah 58:11

Provision

And God is able to make all grace abound to Justin, so that in all things at all times, Justin has all that he needs; Justin will abound in every good work.

2 Corinthians 9:8

And my God will meet all of Justin's needs according to the riches of His glory, Christ Jesus.

Philippians 4:19

His divine power has given Justin everything he needs for life and godliness through his knowledge of Him who called Justin by His own glory and goodness.

2 Peter 1:3

Purity

Create in Justin a clean heart, O God, and renew a right spirit within him.

Psalm 51:10

Blessed is Justin, who is pure in heart, for he will see God.

Matthew 5:8

If Justin confesses his sins, He is faithful and righteous to forgive his sins, and to cleanse Justin from all unrighteousness.

1 John 1:9

Purity

Grace and peace be multiplied unto Justin through the knowledge of God, and of Jesus our Lord. His divine power has granted to Justin all things that pertain to life and godliness, through the knowledge of Him who called Justin to his glory and excellence, by which he has granted to Justin his precious and very great promises, so that through them Justin may become a partaker of the divine nature, having escaped from the corruption that is in the world because of sinful desire.

2 Peter 1:1-4

Redemption

Justin calls upon God, and the Lord saves him. Evening, morning, and at noon, Justin will pray and cry aloud, and God hears his voice. God has redeemed Justin's soul in peace from the battle waged against him.

Psalm 55:16-18

Do not gloat over Justin, enemy! Though Justin has fallen, he will rise; though Justin sits in darkness, the Lord will be his light. Because he has sinned against Him, he will bear the consequences, until He pleads Justin's case and establishes his right. He will bring Justin into the light and Justin will see His righteousness.

Micah 7:8-9

Justin has been crucified with Christ. Justin no longer lives, but Christ lives in him. The life Justin now lives in the body, he lives by faith in the Son of God, who loved him and gave Himself for him.

Galatians 2:20

Revelation

Do not gloat over Justin, enemy! Though Justin has fallen, he will rise; though Justin sits in darkness, the Lord will be his light. Because he has sinned against Him, he will bear the consequences, until He pleads Justin's case and establishes his right. He will bring Justin into the light and Justin will see His righteousness.

Micah 7:8-9

What Justin has received is not the spirit of the world, but the Spirit who is from God, so that he may understand what God has freely given him.

1 Corinthians 2:12

Justin has the mind of Christ and the wisdom of God is formed within him.

1 Corinthians 2:16

Revelation

God, bring to light and remove any darkness in Justin's heart. He will expose any wrong motives to him.

1 Corinthians 4:5

Whenever Justin turns to the Lord, the veil is taken away.

2 Corinthians 3:16

May the Lord Jesus Christ give Justin the Spirit of wisdom and of revelation in the knowledge of Him, having the eyes of his heart enlightened, that Justin may know what is the hope to which He has called him, what are the riches of his glorious inheritance in the saints, and what is the immeasurable greatness of His power toward us who believe, according to the working of His great might.

Ephesians 1:17-19

Righteousness

The Lord dealt with Justin according to his righteousness; according to the cleanness of his hands He rewarded him.

2 Samuel 22:21

Justin clothes himself with the Lord Jesus Christ, and does not think about how to gratify the desires of the flesh.

Romans 13:14

He who supplies seed to the sower and bread for food will supply and multiply Justin's seed for sowing and increase the harvest of his righteousness.

2 Corinthians 9:10

Justin is filled with the fruit of righteousness that comes through Jesus Christ, to the glory and praise of God.

Philippians 1:11

Righteousness

Justin flees the evil desires of his youth and pursues righteousness, faith, love, and peace, along with those who call on the Lord out of a pure heart.

2 Timothy 2:22

Safety & Protection

God is Justin's rock, in whom he takes refuge, his shield and the horn of his salvation. He is Justin's stronghold, his refuge and his savior—from violent people Justin is saved. He calls to the Lord, who is worthy of praise, and Justin is saved from his enemies.

2 Samuel 22:3-4

Justin is safe and hidden in the Lord's shadow away from danger.

Psalm 91:1

Do not withhold Your mercy from Justin, O Lord; may Your love and Your truth always protect him.

Psalm 40:11

The Lord's angels keep charge over Justin to guard him in all his ways.

Psalm 91:11

Safety & Protection

Justin's integrity and uprightness protect him, because Justin's hope, Lord, is in You.

Psalm 25:21

Justin has made the Most High his dwelling place. No harm will befall Justin; no disaster will come near his tent. For He will give His angels charge over Justin to guard him in all of his ways. They will carry him so that Justin does not dash his foot against a stone. They will tread upon the lion and the cobra; they will trample them underfoot. Because Justin loves You, You will deliver him. You will set Justin on high. Justin will call upon You and You will answer him. You will be with Justin in trouble. You will deliver Justin and honor him with a long life. You will satisfy Justin and show him Your salvation.

Psalm 91:9-16

Safety & Protection

When Justin lies down, he will not be afraid; when Justin lies down, his sleep will be sweet. Justin has no fear of sudden disaster or of the ruin that overtakes the wicked, for the Lord is at his side and will keep his foot from being snared.

Proverbs 3:24-26

Justin is taught by the Lord and great will be Justin's peace, his health, safety, protection, and prosperity. In righteousness Justin will be established. Tyranny will be far from Justin; Justin will have nothing to fear. Terror will be far removed; it will not come near Justin. No weapon forged against Justin will prosper.

Isaiah 54:13-14, 17

Justin is afflicted in every way, but not crushed; perplexed, but not driven to despair; persecuted, but not forsaken; struck down, but not destroyed.

2 Corinthians 4:8-9

Salvation

Justin calls upon God, and the Lord saves him. Evening, morning, and at noon, Justin will pray and cry aloud, and God hears his voice. God has redeemed Justin's soul in peace from the battle waged against him.

Psalm 55:16-18

I am convinced that neither death nor life, neither angels nor demons, neither the present nor the future, nor any powers, neither height nor depth, nor anything else in all creation, will be able to separate Justin from the love of God that is in Christ Jesus our Lord.

Romans 8:38-39

Justin confesses with his mouth that Jesus is Lord and Justin believes in his heart that You have raised Christ from the dead. Justin calls on Your name, Lord! Justin is saved as one of Your children.

Romans 10:9-13

Salvation

Justin finds his salvation in repentance and rest. Justin's strength is in quietness and trust.

Isaiah 30:15

Justin is a new creation in Christ Jesus.

2 Corinthians 5:17

Praise be to the God and Father of our Lord Jesus Christ! In His great mercy He has given Justin new birth into a living hope through the resurrection of Jesus Christ from the dead, and into an inheritance that can never perish, spoil, or fade. This inheritance is kept in heaven for Justin, who through faith is shielded by God's power until the coming of the salvation that is ready to be revealed in the last time.

1 Peter 1:3-4

Seeking God

Justin will seek the Lord his God and he will find Him, if he searches after Him with all his heart and with all his soul.

Deuteronomy 4:29

Deal bountifully with Justin, that he may live and keep Your word. Open Justin's eyes that he may behold wondrous things out of the word.

Psalm 119:17-18

O God, You are Justin's God, earnestly he seeks You; Justin's soul thirsts for You, his body longs for You, in a dry and weary land where there is no water. Justin has seen You in the sanctuary and beheld Your power and Your glory. Because Your love is better than life, Justin's lips will glorify You.

Psalm 63:1-3

Seeking God

"I Love Justin who loves me, and as Justin seeks me so he will find me."

Proverbs 8:17

"Justin will call upon me and come and pray to me, and I will hear him. Justin will seek me and find me, when he seeks me with all his heart. I will be found by Justin," declares the Lord.

Jeremiah 29:12-14

The Lord is good to Justin whose hope is in Him, to Justin who seeks Him.

Lamentations 3:25

Justin has the mind of Christ and the wisdom of God is formed within him.

1 Corinthians 2:16

Seeking God

Forgetting what is behind, and straining toward what is ahead, Justin presses on towards the goal to win the prize for which God has called him heavenward in Christ Jesus.

Philippians 3:13-14

Justin draws near to God, and He draws near to him.

James 4:8

Though Justin has not seen Him, he loves Him; and even though Justin does not see Him now, he believes in Him and is filled with an inexpressible and glorious joy, for Justin is receiving the end result of his faith, the salvation of his soul.

1 Peter 1:8-9

Spiritual Growth

He who supplies seed to the sower and bread for food will supply and multiply Justin's seed for sowing and increase the harvest of his righteousness.
2 Corinthians 9:10

Justin, speaking the truth in love, grows up in every way into Him who is the head, into Christ.
Ephesians 4:15

Justin walks in a manner worthy of the Lord, fully pleasing Him, bearing fruit in every good work and growing in the knowledge of God. Justin is strengthened with all power according to His glorious might so that he has great endurance and patience.
Colossians 1:10-11

Justin leaves the elementary doctrine of Christ and goes on to maturity, not laying again the foundation of repentance from dead works and of faith in God.
Hebrews 6:1

Spiritual Growth

Justin is growing in the grace and knowledge of our Lord and savior Jesus Christ. To Him be glory both now and forever! Amen.

2 Peter 3:18

Spiritual Warfare

Justin is strong in the Lord and in his mighty power. Justin puts on the full armor of God, so that he can take his stand against the devil's schemes. For Justin's struggles are not against flesh and blood, but against the rulers, against the authorities, against the powers of this dark world and against the spiritual forces of evil in the heavenly realms. Therefore, Justin puts on the full armor of God, so that when the day of evil comes, Justin will stand his ground. Justin stands firm with the belt of truth buckled around his waist, with the breastplate of righteousness in place, and with his feet fitted with the readiness that comes from the gospel of peace. In addition to all this, Justin takes up the shield of faith, with which he can extinguish all the flaming arrows of the evil one. Justin takes the helmet of salvation and the sword of the Spirit, which is the word of God.

Ephesians 6:10-17

Spiritual Warfare

Justin calls upon God, and the Lord saves him. Evening, morning, and at noon, Justin will pray and cry aloud, and God hears his voice. God has redeemed Justin's soul in peace from the battle waged against him.

Psalm 55:16-18

Justin has authority to trample on snakes and scorpions and to overcome all the power of the enemy; nothing will harm Justin.

Luke 10:19

In all things Justin is more than a conqueror through Him who loved us. For I am convinced that neither death nor life, neither angels nor demons, neither the present nor future, nor any powers, neither height nor depth, nor anything else in all creation, will be able to separate Justin from the love of God that is in Christ Jesus our Lord.

Romans 8:37-39

Spiritual Warfare

Justin is not overcome by evil, but Justin overcomes evil with good.

Romans 12:21

No temptation has overtaken Justin except what is common to mankind. And God is faithful; He will not let Justin be tempted beyond what he can bear. But when Justin is tempted, He will also provide a way out so that he can endure it.

1 Corinthians 10:13

Justin demolishes arguments and every pretension that sets itself up against the knowledge of God, and Justin takes captive every thought and makes it obedient to Christ.

2 Corinthians 10:5

Spiritual Warfare

Justin is delivered from the evils of this present world, for it is the will of God.

Galatians 1:4

Justin is an overcomer and Justin overcomes by the blood of the Lamb and the word of his testimony.

Revelation 12:11

Michelle Leslie

Strength

It is God who arms Justin with strength and makes his way perfect. God makes Justin's feet like the feet of a deer; He enables Justin to stand on the heights.

2 Samuel 22:33-34

The joy of the Lord is Justin's strength. The Lord is the strength of Justin's life.

Nehemiah 8:10

Create in Justin a pure heart, O God, and renew a steadfast spirit within him. Restore to Justin the joy of Your salvation and grant him a willing spirit, to sustain him.

Psalm 51:10,12

Strength

Justin does not walk in the counsel of the ungodly or stand in the path of sinners or sit in the seat of scoffers. But Justin delights himself in the law of the Lord and Justin meditates on His law day and night. Justin is like a tree planted by the rivers of water, which yields its fruit in season and whose leaf will not wither, and whatever he does he prospers.

Psalm 1:1-3

Justin will never be shaken; Justin will be remembered forever. Justin will not fear bad news; his heart is steadfast, trusting in the Lord. Justin's heart is upheld, he will not fear.

Psalm 112:6-8

The Lord makes firm the steps of Justin who delights in him; though Justin stumbles, he will not fall, for the Lord upholds him with His hand.

Psalm 37:23-24

Strength

Justin finds his salvation in repentance and rest. Justin's strength is in quietness and trust.

Isaiah 30:15

Justin hopes in the Lord and the Lord renews his strength. Justin will soar on wings like an eagle. Justin will run and not grow weary. Justin will walk and not be faint.

Isaiah 40:31

Greater is He who is in Justin, than he who is in the world.

1 John 4:4

Justin receives the gift of the Holy Spirit. Justin receives power when the Holy Spirit comes upon him.

Acts 1:8

Justin can do all things through Christ who strengthens him.

Philippians 4:13

Strength

Justin walks in a manner worthy of the Lord, fully pleasing Him, bearing fruit in every good work and growing in the knowledge of God. Justin is strengthened with all power according to His glorious might so that he has great endurance and patience.

Colossians 1:10-11

Just as Justin received Christ Jesus as Lord, he continues to live in Him. Justin is rooted and built up in Him, strengthened in faith as he was taught, and overflowing with thankfulness.

Colossians 2:6-7

The Lord is faithful, and He will strengthen Justin and protect him from the evil one.

2 Thessalonians 3:3

Transformation

Justin delights himself in the Lord and the Lord gives Justin the desires of his heart.

Psalm 37:4

Justin is not conformed to the pattern of this world but he is transformed by the renewing of his mind. Justin's mind is renewed by the word of God.

Romans 12:22

Justin is a new creation in Christ Jesus.

2 Corinthians 5:17

Justin does not lose heart. Though outwardly he is wasting away, yet inwardly Justin is being renewed day by day, for Justin's light and momentary troubles are achieving for him an eternal glory that far outweighs them all. So Justin fixes his eyes not on what is seen, but what is unseen, since what is seen is temporary, but what is unseen is eternal.

2 Corinthians 4:16-18

Transformation

Justin has been crucified with Christ and he no longer lives, but Christ lives in him. The life Justin now lives in the body, he lives by faith in the Son of God, who loved Justin and gave Himself for him.

Galatians 2:20

He who began a good work in Justin will be faithful to complete it.

Philippians 1:6

May God Himself, the God of peace, sanctify Justin through and through. May Justin's whole spirit, soul, and body be kept blameless at the coming of our Lord Jesus Christ.

1 Thessalonians 5:23

Trials

Indeed, Justin felt that he had received the sentence of death. But that was to make him rely not on himself but on God who raises the dead.

2 Corinthians 1:9

And the God of all grace, who called Justin to His eternal glory in Christ, after Justin has suffered a little while, will Himself restore him and make him strong, firm and steadfast.

1 Peter 5:10

In all this Justin greatly rejoices, though now for a little while he may have had to suffer grief in all kinds of trials. These have come so that the proven genuineness of Justin's faith—of greater worth than gold, which perishes even though refined by fire—may result in praise, glory, and honor when Jesus Christ is revealed.

1 Peter 1:6-7

Activating God's Power

Trust

Some trust in chariots and some in horses, but Justin trusts in the name of the Lord our God.

Psalm 20:7

Justin trusts in the Lord with all his heart, and does not lean on his own understanding. In all Justin's ways he acknowledges Him, and He will direct his path.

Proverbs 3:5-6

Justin does not throw away his confident trust in the Lord. Justin is richly rewarded. Justin has patient endurance so that he continues to do God's will. Then Justin will receive all that he has been promised.

Hebrews 10:35-36

Michelle Leslie

Wisdom

The Spirit of the Lord will rest on Justin—the Spirit of wisdom and of understanding, the Spirit of counsel and of might, the Spirit of the knowledge and fear of the Lord.

Isaiah 11:2

I keep asking that the God of our Lord Jesus Christ, the glorious Father, may give Justin the Spirit of wisdom and revelation, so that he may know him better. I pray that the eyes of Justin's heart may be enlightened in order that he may know the hope to which He has called him, the riches of his glorious inheritance in His holy people, and His incomparably great power for us who believe.

Ephesians 1:17-19

And this is my prayer: that Justin's love may abound more and more in knowledge and depth of insight so that Justin may be able to discern what is best and may be pure and blameless until the day of Christ. May Justin be filled with the fruit of righteousness that comes through Jesus Christ to the glory and praise of God.

Philippians 1:9-11

Wisdom

Justin is filled with the knowledge of the Lord's will and all wisdom and spiritual understanding.

Colossians 1:19

When Justin lacks wisdom, he asks God who gives generously to all without finding fault, and it will be given to him.

James 1:5

Worship

Justin trusts in Your unfailing love; his heart rejoices in Your salvation. Justin sings to the Lord, for He has been good to him.

Psalm 13:5-6

In view of God's mercy, Justin offers his body as a living sacrifice, holy and pleasing to God—this is his spiritual act of worship.

Romans 12:1

Justin is grateful for receiving a kingdom that cannot be shaken, and he offers to God acceptable worship, with reverence and awe, for our God is a consuming fire.

Hebrews 12:28-29

Justin fears God and gives Him glory, because the hour of his judgment has come. Justin worships Him who made the heavens, the earth, the sea and the springs of water.

Revelation 14:7

AUTHOR'S NOTE

Biblical reference Hebrews 4:12 says that God's word is alive and powerful, sharper than a two-edged sword. When we speak and pray the Scriptures, we are coming into agreement with God, and His power is released to answer our prayers; and by doing so we strengthen the expression of our prayer. As we pray the word of God we will learn who He is, and who He has made us to be. When we are living in the fullness of our true identity in Christ, we will then experience God and all He has intended for us.

Michelle Leslie

TESTIMONY

It never occurred to me that I would write a book. This was not a secret dream or desire. It was in a desperate moment of brokenness and confusion that the Holy Spirit led me to write my first book of prayers for my husband Peter and I. I was in a season of many tears, anxiety, and barely any sleep. To say I was lost is an understatement! All I knew was that I was a woman committed to her marriage through God, and yet I found myself separated from my husband after being divorced and remarried… again.

I felt regret, failure, fear, exhaustion, and sadness. Somehow, having been in this situation before didn't help any. In fact it made me feel worse. My prayer life was barely alive because I found myself in such a pathetic state. Sometimes all I could pray was "I trust You, Lord." Being so empty, this statement was all I had to offer. I was so messed up that it felt like I said it every thirty seconds.

Activating God's Power

I entered into a season in which the Lord told me not to talk to my husband. All of our conversations were leading to more division. The only way God allowed me to contact Peter was by sending him loving or encouraging text messages and scriptures. He also led me to start writing scriptures down and inserting our names into them. Although still broken, my prayers were empowered. I was praying God's will for our lives. I was unleashing the power of the Holy Spirit into my marriage. I wrote these scriptures on little white spiral-bound note cards. This task sustained me through a terrible time, transformed both of our hearts, and I believe it brought my husband and I back together.

I understand that not all trials end in victory. Because Peter and I are human, we will have struggles again. But I will never stop using the gift that God gave me. It changes me continually. And during the time I described above the prayers enabled me to function as a mom in an upside-down world.

I soon realized the power these little books had and started writing them for my children and for the people around me who were going through tough times. The response was unbelievable. I heard things like "This is just what I needed," and many stories of hope and change.

If you are looking to grow in your relationship with God or to overcome a difficult situation, I encourage you to pray this little book and to pray it for those you love. Get ready to be transformed and to be a world changer. Life will never be the same.

ABOUT THE AUTHOR

Michelle Leslie was raised in rural Oregon. She is a pillar of activation within the Body of Christ with a heart to hear God's word and see it lived out as her calling and destiny. Along with her gift for challenging people to be all they were created to be in their life, she is a fun-loving, hard-working, creative friend, daughter, mom, and wife.

As a child, Michelle was dyslexic. Because of her trouble learning to read, she struggled through every subject in school and was doomed to special education classes (which she perceived as "social suicide"). When Michelle came to know the Lord in her early twenties she was desperate for God's word. As she dove into the word of God, her life changed dramatically. Romans 12:2 was in full effect, and Michelle was transformed by the renewing of her mind. The effects of the learning disability that had held Michelle back her whole life were slowly diminishing. Michelle was finally reading and retaining information, growing in confidence, and developing a voice for the message God had given her to share. God's power was being made perfect in her weakness, and through this platform God demonstrated his love and transforming power to those around her.

Michelle has a deep desire for others to experience the transformation and freedom that can only be found in Christ, and she is sharing it with all who will listen through this extraordinary upcoming book, *Activating God's Power*.

Michelle is writing in the hope of meeting the needs of readers in desperation, or those who are seeking spiritual growth in themselves or in their loved ones. Michelle lives in Denver, Colorado with her husband and two daughters.

CONTACT

To order books please see instructions at:
www.MichelleLeslie.net

To contact Michelle Leslie directly:
Michelle@MichelleLeslie.net

Follow Michelle Leslie online:

Facebook.com/MichelleLeslie.net

@MichelleLeslie_

MichelleLeslie_

Made in the USA
Monee, IL
25 June 2025